THE
SPIRIT *of*
SERVANTHOOD

THE SPIRIT *of* SERVANTHOOD

Victor Ansor

CHALFANT ECKERT
PUBLISHING

The Spirit of Servanthood

Copyright © 2015 Victor Ansor. All Rights Reserved.

No rights claimed for public domain material, all rights reserved. No parts of this publication may be reproduced, stored in any retrieval system, or transmitted in any form or by any means, electronic, mechanical, recording, or otherwise, without the prior written permission of the author. Violations may be subject to civil or criminal penalties.

Library of Congress Control Number: 2015951910

ISBN: 978-1-63308-173-4 (paperback)
ISBN: 978-1-63308-174-1 (ebook)

Interior Design by R'tor John D. Maghuyop
Cover Illustration by Miša Jovanović

CHALFANT ECKERT
PUBLISHING

1028 S Bishop Avenue, Dept. 178
Rolla, MO 65401

Printed in the United States of America

To my mother, Agatha.

To Dr. David O. Oyedepo,

who taught me how to serve God.

TABLE OF CONTENTS

The Mandate 9
Introduction 11
Anchor Scripture 15
Who Is a Servant? 17
There Is a Spirit of Servanthood 23
Whom to Serve 29
How to Serve 33
Channels of Service 45
Where to Serve 53
Service Is a Choice 59
Eye Service 63
Mother of All Service 69
Human Worship 77
Reputation Consciousness 81
Pride, the Bane of Servanthood 85
The Place of Obedience 91
Service: The Pathway to Greatness 99
Moment of Decision 117
How to Get the Spirit of Servanthood 119
Benefits of Kingdom Service 125
Epilogue 141

THE MANDATE

EPHESIANS 3:8-11

Unto me, who am less than the least
of all saints, is this grace given, that
I should preach among the Gentiles
the unsearchable riches of Christ; and
to make all men see what is the fellowship
of the mystery, which from the
beginning of the world had been hid
in God, who created all things by Jesus
Christ: To the intent that now unto the
principalities and powers in heavenly
places might be known by the church
the manifold wisdom of God, according
to the eternal purpose which he
purposed in Christ Jesus our Lord.

INTRODUCTION

There is a vital spirit in the kingdom of God that either has been ignored or outright forgotten by believers. This spirit is responsible for kingdom service, and without this spirit we as Christians cannot serve God effectively. Many people started out with zeal after new birth to serve God in diverse capacities, but they are nowhere to be found today. Many of these servants of God, or at least that is what we are calling them, are either tired, worn out, or simply reluctant to continue in their service in the vineyard of God.

In every endeavor of life, there is a driving force. Something that pushes you and makes you do what you want to do so you can get to where you want to go. This force acts as a catalyst in helping you achieve your goals. In God's kingdom, this is no exception, which is why God has provided a driving force to help us serve him effectively and tirelessly.

ISAIAH 42:1-4

Behold my servant, whom I uphold;
mine elect, in whom my soul delighted;
**I have put my spirit upon him...
He shall not fail nor be discouraged...**

In my course of service to God since I gave my life to Jesus, I have come to understand that I cannot do the things I am doing in God's house without empowerment. Sometimes people ask me, "Aren't you tired?" My answer is always "no" because I have never been tired of doing His work.

I did not know what my driving force was until Bishop David Oyedepo, who is my father in the Lord, opened my eyes in one of our meetings and introduced the spirit to me. I will say with all sense of humility that the first spirit I encountered when I came to Jesus was the *Spirit of Servanthood*. I believe God baptized me with this spirit to take me to my next level. Since then, I have been changing levels dramatically. This is the spirit I want to introduce you to in this book, and I believe as you read, God will baptize you with this awesome spirit and your life will not be the same.

In the church today, people are interested in positions, titles, and occupying a seat, but nobody wants to serve.

MATTHEW 21:23

> Then came to him the mother of Zebedee's children with her sons, worshipping him, and desiring a certain thing of him. And he said unto her, what wilt thou? She said unto him, grant that these my two sons may sit, the one on thy right hand, and the other on the left, in thy kingdom.

Apostles James and John brought their mother to Jesus to seek positions for them. Perhaps they thought that because they may not be able to get what they want by themselves, maybe bringing their mother, who may have been an influential society lady at the time, might get it for them. Their mother came and requested of Jesus that he should make her two sons to sit one on the right and the other on the left. I wonder how other disciples may have looked at them when she made such a request. Imagine it, they had to bring their mother to make a request for them! James and John were looking for position and not opportunity to serve.

The same thing is happening in church today: people want position, they want to be recognized. People have gone to great lengths to get positions in church today. They don't know that the way to the top is from the ground. You have to serve first before you can be served. Therefore, by the help of the Holy Spirit, I will be showing you what servanthood truly means and why we are called to serve. God bless you as you take this journey with me.

ANCHOR SCRIPTURE

ISAIAH 42:1-4

Behold **my servant**, whom I uphold;
mine elect, in whom my soul delighted;
I have put my spirit upon him: he shall
bring forth judgment to the Gentiles.
He shall not cry, nor lift up, nor cause
his voice to be heard in the street.
A bruised reed shall he not break, and
the smoking flax shall he not quench:
he shall bring forth judgment unto
truth. **He shall not fail nor be discouraged,**
till he have set judgment in the earth:
and the isles shall wait for his law.

WHO IS A SERVANT?

MARK 10:42-45

But Jesus called them to him and said unto them, ye know that they which are accounted to rule over the Gentiles exercise lordship over them; and their great ones exercise authority upon them. But so shall it not be among you: But whosoever will be great among you, shall be your minister: And whosoever of you will be the chiefest, shall be servant of all. For even the son of man came not to be ministered unto, but to minister, and to give his life a ransom for many.

A servant is one who serves.

A servant could also mean someone who voluntarily dedicates himself or herself to the service of another. Throughout the Bible, we see people who dedicated themselves to the service of

God or a particular man. Being a servant does not mean you are less of a human, but rather that you show strength and leadership.

In this age where everyone wants to be served, those who serve are actually the ones in control. Let's use this secular example. A driver who drives his boss is actually the one in control of the car. He enjoys the car more than the owner who bought it. He knows everything about the car. He takes his boss from one spot to the other, but he is the one who feels the car more than the owner. You may see him as a common driver, but he is actually more in tune with the car and enjoys the car more than the owner of the car. Servants are actually in control.

Jesus Christ, our example of a true servant, made it clear in Luke 22:27:

> …but I am among you as
> he that serveth.

A true servant is a true follower. You cannot be a good leader without first being a good follower, so a good follower is a true servant and eventually a great leader. This thing we call leadership actually means to serve. That is why I get so mad at people who reduce themselves to beggars just to get something from the politicians they elected to serve them. It is a lack of understanding that makes people feel they are at the mercy of their leaders. The people you elect into office are actually your servants. Title or position either in church or in the secular world does not make a leader; it is service that makes a leader. Not many people today are servants; most want to be served.

In the body of Christ, we see people lording over one another, especially when they are given titles. People do all kinds of dubious things just to get a title, and this title makes them sit as lords in God's house where they are supposed to be serving. It is in church that we find more lords than in the outside world. As soon as you give them a title, they begin to puff up. Some don't even tolerate you calling them by their name, insisting you use their title, and if you keep calling them by their name, they will not talk to you anymore because they feel insulted that you don't recognize their position. These kinds of people are not servants.

MARK 10:42-45

> But Jesus called them to him and said unto them, ye know that they which are accounted to rule over the Gentiles exercise lordship over them; and their great ones exercise authority upon them. But so shall

> it not be among you: But whosoever will be great among you, shall be your minister: And whosoever of you will be the chiefest, shall be servant of all. For even the son of man came not to be ministered unto, but to minister, and to give his life a ransom for many.

Here, Jesus clearly explains what servanthood means. He makes us understand that to be great you must serve, for leadership means serving others. Contrary to biblical principles, church leaders have constituted themselves into lords and kings who sit and give orders to their subjects; title holders who are supposed to render service to the flocks are now demanding honor, worship, and service. A church leader once told me that I didn't show respect to him and I said in my heart that if this man starts demanding respect, then there is a problem.

We have been called to serve, not to be served. A servant always serves, and serving does not mean you bring yourself low, but is a show of greatness. The body of Christ needs to understand this so they don't continue to walk in error. Jesus, the son of the living God, lived in heaven but came down to the earth as one hundred percent God and one hundred percent man. He still served. Then how about we who are humans? When we serve, we will not only reflect the nature of Christ, we will end up showing true greatness. A servant does not preach and demand money or "prophets offering" as they call it. Anyone who asks you for prophets offering is not a servant of God.

There are many terrible things going on in the body of Christ that show that many of those who call themselves God's servants are actually wolves in sheep's clothing. They parade themselves as men of God but are going around seeking unsuspecting people whom they can deceive and extort from in the name of Christ. If a preacher asks you to give a specific amount of money that you don't have, he is a liar. God will never ask you to bring what he has not given to you. A true servant of God will not go about deceiving and defrauding people, but will nurture and preserve every sheep that God has given to him to care for. I hear and read about pastors who are involved in armed robberies, prostitution rings, heists, and all kinds of fraud just to make money and live large; they are not servants of God. Their deeds bring shame to the name of God and constantly make the enemy point accusing fingers and blaspheme.

2 SAMUEL 12:14

Howbeit, because by this deed thou
has given great occasion to the enemies
of the LORD to blaspheme...

If God called you to serve him but instead, you decide to use the platform to perpetrate evil, you have brought shame to the name of God. A servant is not greater than his master and Jesus is our master. Therefore, if you call yourself God's servant, you must be willing to follow his instructions and leading. A servant is humble, ever ready to serve and loyal to his master.

THERE IS A SPIRIT OF SERVANTHOOD

ISAIAH 42:1

Behold my servant, whom I uphold;
mine elect, in whom my soul delighted;
I have put my spirit upon him...

There is a spirit called the spirit of servanthood.

One of the vital spirits in the kingdom is the spirit of servanthood; this spirit is barely known by believers because it is not frequently introduced. The spirit of servanthood is the force behind kingdom service; for every child of God to serve God effectively, he or she must receive this spirit.

The spirit of servanthood is an attribute of the Holy Spirit, just like the spirit of holiness, adoption, love, power, and sound mind, according to Romans 1:4, 8:15 and 1 Timothy 1:7. We can only serve by the help of the spirit and without the spirit, the service will be empty religious activities. Without the spirit, even if you are a Bishop, His Holiness, Venerable or Holy Father, it will all be a waste of time. Many people in church today are only filling position and engaging in activities. That is why there is nothing to show for all their efforts. It is the Holy Spirit that works miracles in the church. A church without the Spirit is an empty church; there will be no miracle, no tangible proof, of what is being preached.

Where there is no operation of the spirit of servanthood, you will find people forming cliques, engaging in backbiting, slandering, tribalism, hatred, anger, pride, rancor, and quarrel. I recently read a story about two pastors from a Pentecostal church fighting on a Sunday morning about control of the church. The police had to intervene and close the church, and the two pastors were taken to the police station for questioning. This is a church with over a thousand members. That is shameful. It goes to show that they are businessmen who engage in religious activities for selfish interests. They do not have the Spirit working in them, for where the Spirit of God is, there is liberty (2 Corinthians 3:17). You can't have the spirit of servanthood and be fighting for position and control in God's house. It is the spirit of servanthood that enables us to serve.

I was introduced into kingdom service five months after rededicating my life to Jesus. It all started one early Saturday morning when I got to my church program and I decided to use the bathroom. I saw a group of people sweeping and washing the toilets and they were doing it with smiles and dancing in the process. I looked at them with dismay and wondered what is so special about washing the bathroom and sweeping the floor. When I finished and walked outside, a voice said to me quietly in my heart, "Join them." I couldn't believe what I heard and I started asking why I should be washing the bathroom when I am supposed to sit down in the congregation and hear the word. But the voice was so strong and I started feeling good about it inside of me, so I met the leader of the group and that is how I ended up in the sanctuary keepers unit of my church.

The interesting thing is, since I joined that group and got baptized in the Holy Ghost, I have never been tired of going to clean the church no matter the weather or how I felt. I have awakened at 4 a.m. in Ghana and started trekking miles just to meet up cleaning. I have passed through some dangerous places where kidnappers and armed robbers are predominant just to go to church and clean. In most cases I am always the first to be in church, and many thought I just live around the corner only to be surprised one day that where I live is actually miles away.

The spirit of servanthood is what motivates you to serve God; the spirit will not allow you to sit down in church when there are things to do. It is the spirit that moves you to go to church even when you don't feel like it.

In my own case, I will tell you the truth; there are times I don't feel like going to church, yet I can't stay away. I am too involved in my church to a point that many complain to my face that I am everywhere. "You carry this thing too much on your head," some said. A deacon once told me, "Don't worry, you will soon get tired one day. I started like you and now I am relaxed."

One day it was raining heavily on my way to church, and I had to branch under a shade to wait for the rain to subside. For the next thirty minutes the rain did not show any sign of stopping and the day was breaking. Since I had to be in church early to arrange and wipe the chairs for the Sunday service before people came, I entered that heavy rain and I was soaked inside out. I eventually got to church wet, yet I still cleaned the chairs and sat throughout the service in wet clothes and I was not discouraged.

From our anchor Scripture in Isaiah 42:1:

> **Behold my servant**, whom I uphold;
> mine elect, in whom my soul delighted;
> **I have put my spirit upon him...**

THE SPIRIT OF SERVANTHOOD

We see that God puts his spirit upon his servant; this spirit is not for lords but for servants. When you are baptized with the spirit of servanthood, you serve God effectively. It is the spirit of servanthood that empowers you to serve, not money or reward. The way I serve God in my church made one of my unit leaders call me one day and ask, "How much are they paying you?" I was pained by the question because I did not believe a leader would wonder how much I am being paid to do all that I have been doing. The spirit of servanthood makes you do things for God so that others begin to wonder how much you are being paid to do it.

One day I was asked to join in taking the church truck to go and buy stuff for the food pantry. We spent the whole day shopping and loading and offloading the truck, and while we were rounding up, the head of that group asked me how much I wanted to be paid and I quickly answered, "Far be it from me that I should take money from the church; I came to serve." Everyone looked at me with surprise. Why should I accept money? How can I come to serve and expect to be paid? The spirit of servanthood makes you do things that others think impossible.

The spirit of servanthood is one of the spirits that was given to Jesus for his earthly ministry; this spirit, I believe, is what helped him to accomplish his task.

The night Jesus was to be arrested, we saw him praying for the cup to be taken from him, but he made one remarkable statement in Luke 22:42, saying,

> Father, if thou be willing, remove this cup from me: **nevertheless not my will, but thine, be done.**

A servant will always want the will of his master to be done; he will never argue or show insubordination. Jesus showed this example by telling God that he was afraid and would prefer not to continue, but his Father's will should be done. The spirit of servanthood kept Jesus going. That is why he did not give up despite the prevailing circumstance.

The spirit of servanthood is what will make you not steal from the church if you are given the opportunity to be counting church money. It is the spirit that will make you not put your hand into the church treasury to take money for your personal use even if you are the founder of that church. When this spirit comes on you, you will be diligent, prudent, effective, and sincere in all your dealings in God's house. There is a spirit called the spirit of servanthood, and I pray that you will be baptized with this spirit in Jesus' name.

WHOM TO SERVE

LUKE 4:8

And Jesus answered and said unto him, Get thee behind me, Satan: for it is written, Thou shalt worship the Lord thy God, **and him only shall thou serve**.

Our service is to God.

In every institution or organization, there is always the head that everyone works for. When we wake up in the morning and rush to work, there is someone whom we must report to, but ultimately all of our service is to God no matter who our boss is. Many Christians think that their service in the church is for the pastor or the leader to whom they report; no, our service in the church is unto God. Many do not know this, and that is why they walk in error. Everything we do in the house of God is to the glory of God.

LUKE 4:8

And Jesus answered and said unto him, Get thee behind me, Satan: for it is written, Thou shalt worship the Lord thy God, and **him only shall thou serve**.

Many of us in the body of Christ are busy serving people while thinking that we are serving God. The above Scripture says that it is only God that we should serve, so our service is to the one and only true God and not to man. In every service, the Scripture says that we should do it as unto God. That means God expects us to render service in whatever dimension as unto him.

COLOSSIANS 3:23

And whatsoever ye do, do it heartily, as to the Lord, and not unto men.

This means that in whatever responsibility we are entrusted in the church, we should do it as though God is the one we are reporting to. We should not think it is for the people we see or for those who gave us the responsibility, but we should do it as unto God.

In our secular responsibilities, we should do them as if we are doing them unto God, whether in our job, career, business, or whatever it may be. When we work as though God is our employer, we will give our best and from there we will unconsciously release our full potential. This I believe will please God and will make him work through us and make us a showpiece on the earth. When we serve as though we are serving God, we will not take whatever we do for granted; we will not be on the phone when we are supposed to be working.

There are people who go to work but spend the greater part of their work day browsing through Facebook, Twitter, and Whatsup. This is unacceptable because God does not like that. When you go to work, know that you are there to serve. When you did not have that job, you were bombarding heaven day and night with prayer for a job and now that you have it, you are wasting precious job hours doing things that will not bring any benefit or growth to that establishment. We should understand one thing; that what we do at our job will either help build it or destroy it. If you spend that time you waste on the internet in productive thinking while serving at your job, you may come up with an idea that may turn that establishment around for good.

If you are a pastor, serve with all your heart knowing that you are doing it unto God, whether you are paid well or not, whether you are posted to a good location with thousands of members or not. As a church board chairman or unit head, serve God in that position; don't use it to oppress people. No matter whom we report to in our service, we should know that God is the one we serve.

HOW TO SERVE

PSALM 100:2

Serve the LORD with gladness:
come before his presence with singing.

There is how-to in everything that we do, and in God's service this is no exception. When we come to serve God we must know how to serve him; otherwise, we may not reap the fruit of that service.

SERVE IN LOVE

In everything we do, let it be done in love. If we don't serve in love, we are not serving at all. If you truly love God, you will love people. You can't claim to love God when you are at variance with people. One day I went to serve in my unit, which is cleaning the bathroom and preparing it for Sunday service. My church sits fifty thousand worshippers in four services; it is widely acclaimed to be the largest church in the world. You will understand it means so much for us to come on a Saturday to prepare it for thousands of worshippers that will troop in the next day.

I was almost done cleaning when a young man came in with mud on his shoes and requested to use the place. I was furious because he came in and dirtied the place I had done cleaning, and I almost did not allow him to enter to use the bathroom. When the head of my unit came in, he saw the mud and understood that I didn't want the young man to use the bathroom, so he smiled and said, "Let him use it, Victor, the bathroom was made for man and not man for the bathroom. He is the reason why we are here to clean. Let him give you more work to do so God can pay you overtime." That day, I learned that we are to love people. I was serving, but I did not do it with love and that is why I was going to refuse that child of God from using the bathroom. I know people can be very mean, but we must love.

ROMAN 13:10

Love worketh no ill to his neighbor:
therefore love is the fulfilling of the law.

You are not serving in love if you are oppressive, mean, vindictive, cruel, or bossy. In our primary place of assignment, we must show love to those around us and render our service as though it is to God. No matter what people have done to us, we must forgive and move on. Whatever you are called to do, do it in love and your reward shall be great. No matter what they say about you, love them. When you serve God with love in your heart, no matter the gang up against you, God will so bless you and will take you higher above where they will have to lift up their eyes to locate you. You will give great testimonies while they are still at the same level. Genuine lovers of God are servants of God.

SERVE WITH JOY

In service to God, we must learn to do it with joy. A sad face does not intimidate God; neither will it bring anything good to us. When we come to serve God, we must put up a joyful countenance knowing that he has not called us to serve him in vain.

ISAIAH 45:19

> I have not spoken in secret, in a dark place of the earth: **I said not unto the seed of Jacob, seek ye me in vain:** I the LORD speak righteousness, I declare things that are right.

If you are sad, I will say it is better to sort out yourself before you do anything in God's name. Be joyful in your primary place of assignment, for this is a sickle to the harvest of blessing. Even at your job, business, or career, try to put up a smile. Be joyful even if you are not paid well or it is not the kind of job you should be doing.

NEHEMIAH 2:1-2

And it came to pass in the month Nisan, in the twentieth year of Artaxerxes the king, that wine was before him: and I took up the wine, and gave it unto the king. Now I had not been beforetime sad in his presence. Wherefore the king said unto me, Why is thy countenance sad, seeing thou art not sick? This is nothing else but sorrow of heart. Then I was very sore afraid.

Nehemiah was serving the king of Babylon then as someone who poured wine into the cup for the king to drink. This was a delicate job because the life of the king was in his hands. Someone could have easily paid Nehemiah to poison the king, and in those days, especially someone with that kind of job wouldn't appear before the king looking sad. That would have spelled doom because the king would feel uncomfortable, thinking Nehemiah was planning something against him, and he could command that Nehemiah be killed. If that could be the case with a king who is a man, how about the King of kings,

God? If you can't appear before a king looking sad, you should not appear before God looking sad.

Lack of joy makes us lose out in receiving our blessing. God is a generous employer and over the years I have seen that he pays more than any corporation on the earth. No matter what you face in life, no matter how the enemy has battered you and things do not yet work out the way you want, when you come to God's presence or in your primary place of assignment, fill your heart with joy, try to put up a smile, and tell the devil he cannot steal your joy; you will serve God with joy today. I know life can be very hard and our desires seem to be far from being realized. I know man may have offended you and pushed you to the wall and everything may have turn upside down, but let nothing steal your joy, for therein lies your reward. Learn to look beyond the horizon for in every dark tunnel, there is a glimpse of light at the end.

HEBREW 12:2

Looking unto Jesus the author
and finisher of our faith; who
for the **joy** that was set before him
endured the cross, and despising
the shame, and is set down at
the right hand of the throne of God

Look beyond the circumstance and everything that is manifesting in the negative. Know that since Jesus overcame, you too will. There is always test and trial before beauty. God is with you and you will overcome; therefore, serve with joy.

Serve with Praise

PSALM 22:3

> But thou art holy, O thou that
> inhabitest the praises of Israel.

When you form an attitude of praising God in your primary place of assignment, you are invoking God's presence. When I joined the sanctuary unit of my church and was sent to wash bathrooms, flush the toilets, and mop the floor, I was taught to do it praising God. They told me that "a closed mouth is a closed destiny" so I should give glory to God while doing it and I will see God manifest in my life.

I rededicated my life to Jesus and came into the church with so many ailments. I was diagnosed with a severe kidney infection; I was also diagnosed with enteritis and I was born with chronic malaria and chronic chest pain. I was always sick with an ulcer and typhoid among other ailments. So when I go to wash the bathroom, I will play music on my phone and be singing as I was taught; sometimes I will pause a little to dance. It was a very ridiculous thing to do, and at first I was ashamed doing it, but I had no choice than to join in since everybody was doing the same. Bishop David Oyedepo said, "It is foolishness to be shameful of what is gainful." He also said, "If you do the ridiculous, you will see the miraculous." So I joined in doing the ridiculous, and after some months, I saw the miraculous.

I used to live on drugs, especially for malaria, and I forgot to take my drugs and I did not go to the hospital for almost a year. One day, I heard someone talk about the hospital and it quickly dawned on me that I had not visited the hospital for a long time and the symptoms of all the sicknesses had disappeared, praise God. This should make you understand that when you praise God while serving him, he takes care of things concerning you. I must tell you for five years now since I joined the sanctuary unit and doing it faithfully, I have not been sick. Sometimes I will go to clean the church and am not happy but before I finish cleaning, that heaviness will be taken away. Praise God while you serve him and he will show up.

SERVE WITH EXPECTATION

As you serve God in any capacity, expect something from him. Know that God is a generous employer and that he doesn't use people; instead, he blesses them. You can tie that service to a particular need and expect God to intervene.

PSALM 123:2

> Behold as the eyes of servants look
> unto the hand of their masters, and
> as the eyes of a maiden unto the hand
> of her mistress; so our eyes wait upon
> the LORD our God, until that he have
> mercy upon us.

Do not serve God without any expectation in your heart, for expectation is the mother of manifestation. Expect to get that promotion at your job by tying it to that particular service. If you need the fruit of the womb, tie it to your service. I told you how I was healed of diverse sicknesses but here is how; when I go to wash the bathroom, while washing the toilet I will say, "Jesus, as I wash this toilet, wash my life from every filth," and when I am about to flush the toilet, I will say, "Jesus, as I flush this toilet, please flush anything that you have not planted in my life." I kept saying those words not knowing that sicknesses were being flushed away from me as I was saying it till it was all gone. I always go to clean with expectation. Don't go to do anything without expecting anything from God your father unless you don't have any need.

Serve Diligently

Serve God diligently. Do God's work as if it is your business that you want to succeed. Be very committed with your service to God; serve him as if your life depends on it. Don't do God's work casually or whenever you like as if it doesn't bother you. Don't finish your own work before you remember there is a church assignment waiting for you. Remember that God watches everything we do; give your all to it. I have seen pastors who are in the habit of coming to church late and I always ask myself, if these pastors were so committed to God's work, would they come late? If it is their business, they will show up on time so they won't lose a client but when it comes to God's work, they take it for granted. If you are committed to God's work, he will be committed to your work also. I always believe that the way we treat God's work is the way he treats our welfare. When it concerns God, be serious about it. Work hard to move the kingdom of God forward, for this is diligence, and watch out how God will make sure you are rewarded.

ROMANS 12:11

Not slothful in businesses; fervent in spirit; serving the Lord.

Inasmuch as we are not to slack in doing our business, we are not to be slothful in doing our service to God. As we are fervent in spirit, we should also be diligent in God's work. Learn to work hard for God. Put God's work first before everything. Let God's calendar determine how your work schedule is and not the reverse. When you serve diligently, you have not only shown how your life should be ordered, you are a true servant of God.

Serve Passionately

Be passionate about God's work and he will be passionate about your affairs. Be sure to serve with all your heart. When you are passionate about something, it always shows in your attitude toward that thing. I am an addicted servant of God and I serve with all my heart; that is why I can't do eye service. I take God's work as my business and since I can't let my business fail, therefore I can't allow the work of God to fail. I have refused some kinds of jobs simply because they would interfere with my service in the house of God. I was offered a very good job with a very good pay, and during the interview, I told them that I have to close early on Wednesdays so I can go to church in time. I also refuse to work on Saturday because I have to be in church to clean, and Sunday is completely out because I can't miss it for anything. They all look at me like a fool and ask, "Where in America would someone like you be employed with all these religious excuses?" I laughed and left, yet I have never been stranded or lacked once. When you are passionate about God's work, he will be passionate about your welfare. Some people take jobs even on Sundays and still count that as a blessing; some who were passionate about kingdom service when they were jobless suddenly lost the passion to serve at the slightest employment opportunity that came their way.

CHANNELS OF SERVICE

EPHESIANS 4:11-12

And he gave some, apostles;
and some, prophets;
and some, evangelists; and some,
pastors and teachers;
For the perfecting of the saints,
for the work of the
ministry, for the edifying of
the body of Christ.

ACT 6:2 AND 4

Then the twelve called the multitude
of the disciples unto them, and said,
it is not reason that we should leave
the word of God, and serve tables...
But we will give ourselves continually
to prayer, and to the ministry of **the word**.

There are channels of service in the kingdom.

We have been called to serve and God has given us different capacities to serve him. In our context of kingdom service, there are ways which we can serve God; these are spiritual services and practical services. Spiritual services include praise and worship, prayer and fasting, and ministry of the word, while practical services include serving God with our intellect, time, energy, and resources.

Spiritual Service

The number one way to serve God is through spiritual service. When you are baptized with the spirit of servanthood, you will serve God by:

Worship

The spirit of servanthood enables you to serve God by worshipping him. This spirit makes you acknowledge God as the Supreme Being to whom all glory belongs. You can wake up at night and begin to sing praise to God. It is the spirit of servanthood that makes you live a praiseful lifestyle. You can't be a true servant of God without being a praise addict. The Bible records how King David, a praise addict and a true servant of God, was praising God seven times a day.

THE SPIRIT OF SERVANTHOOD

PSALM 119:164

Seven times a day do I praise
thee because of thy righteous
judgments.

When you worship God, you are rendering spiritual service to him. A true servant of God will always praise God for who he is and not for what he did. If David, who was a king, could praise God seven times, when did he have time to do other things that were required of him as a king? When that spirit comes upon you, you will worship God no matter the circumstance or situation you find yourself.

We see the story of Paul and Silas, who were arrested and jailed to be killed the next day. Instead of being filled with fear and beginning to ask God why, they switched to praise. They did not allow the situation to control them, and neither did they murmur and complain; rather, they began to sing praises to God and we all know what happened next.

ACT 16:25

And at midnight Paul and Silas
prayed, and sang praises unto God:
and the prisoners heard them.

Worshipping God in any situation shows that you are a true servant who trusts absolutely in him, not minding whatever you may be facing.

Prayer and Fasting

You can serve God through prayer and fasting.

We know the story of Anna, a widow whom the Bible records as always being in the temple serving God in prayer and fasting.

> LUKE 2:36-37
>
> And there was one Anna, a prophetess, the daughter of Phanuel, of the tribe of Aser: she was of a great age, and had lived with an husband seven years from her virginity; and she was a widow of about fourscore and four years, which departed not from the temple, but served God with fastings and prayers night and day.

The case of Anna is a true example of serving God in prayer and fasting, but this can be done through the empowerment of the spirit of servanthood. This spirit will enable you to fast and pray for the things of the kingdom. You can say, "But I have been fasting and praying." Yes, that is true, but a kind of selfish service when you fast and pray for yourself. When you decide to fast and pray for the things of the kingdom and the advancement of God's kingdom on the earth, you are rendering spiritual service.

You can fast and pray for the leadership of your church no matter how big or small it may be. You can fast and pray for souls to be saved. You can also fast and pray against any incursion of hell that is working against the advancement of the church of Christ on the earth. This is what we call spiritual services.

Ministry of the Word

In the book of Acts, the apostles made a clear distinction between spiritual service and practical service. There was a need in the church, but the Apostles knew what they were called to do so they had to clearly state it and also what others should be doing in order to serve God effectively

ACT 6:2 AND 4

> Then the twelve called the multitude
> of the disciples unto them, and said,
> it is not reason that we should leave
> the word of God, and serve tables...
> But we will give ourselves continually
> to prayer, and to the ministry of **the word**.

The apostles knew that God did not call them to serve food but to minister spiritual food, which is the word of God; they had to distance themselves from it to avoid error. When you labor in the word of God, you are doing spiritual service. You study the word and then minister to people. When a pastor stands to preach in a church service, he is doing spiritual service. During sermons in church, there are diverse visitations from the throne of grace, and God, through the pastor, will minister to the needs of the people.

Practical Service

Serving God with Your Intellect

This aspect of service is practical service to God using your intellect; making use of your skills and expertise in advancing the kingdom of Christ. Whatever you know to do that is a need in your primary place of worship, can be done by you. If you are an accountant, and your church has need of an accountant, instead of asking for higher pay so you can work for them, choose a day when you are free then come and volunteer to do it for free. If you are a computer expert, you can help out in your church to fill that need. This is practical service. If you are knowledgeable in any area or field of study, you can use it to serve God in your local assembly without demanding to be paid.

Time and Energy

You can serve God with your time and energy by belonging to any service unit in your church. I don't think there is a church these days that doesn't have a serving unit. Find somewhere in your church where you can serve God passionately and with commitment. Don't sit down in a church when there are things to be done. You can join the choir if you know how to sing. You can join the sanctuary unit and clean the church. The ushering department is there; be a part of it. How can you be in a church with all your strength and energy and yet your church will pay people to come and clean it; why should you allow that to happen in your lifetime? Use your strength to serve God and see him decorate your life. I always feel so happy when I see people in church taking care of the traffic, security, protocol, and hospitality; they come to church not to sit down but to serve. There is a unit in church for everyone; find one that suits you and join.

Financial Resources

You can serve God with your finances. If God has blessed you and you see a need in your church, take care of it. That is service. Look around your local church and see if there is a use for the finances God has blessed you with. Your church does not need to make an announcement or do fundraising to get something done when you alone can foot the bill. If you don't see any need or don't know what to do, write some checks and give them to the church to use when any need arises. Be a giver; don't hoard the resources God has given you. When you serve God with your finances, he blesses you the more. There are children in your church who can't afford an education; help them pay for it. If there is a job opening in your place of work, inform members of your church so they can have the opportunity to be empowered financially. Be a blessing.

WHERE TO SERVE

DEUTERONOMY 12:13-14

Take heed to thyself that thou
offer not thy burnt offerings in
every place that thou seest:
But in the place which the LORD
shall choose in one of thy tribes,
there thou shall offer thy burnt
offerings, and there thou shall
do all that I command thee.

Your Local Assembly

There is a place of service and God will always meet you at your place of service.

You cannot work in the United Nations and collect your wages at the White House. Where you are fed spiritually and consistently is your place of service. You cannot be a member of the Methodist church, and every weekend you go to the Presbyterian church to help them clean the church. Where you have been planted is your place of service. Be a part of what is going on in your church; be fully involved. Serve God in your local church.

Be an active member and not a passive one. Don't be a religious prostitute, going from one place to another thinking you are doing service to God. That doesn't mean you can't be a blessing to another church, but your first port of call is your local church. If your local church has a need or function that requires you to be there, don't say your brother or sister wants you to go and help in their church. Your primary responsibility is to help in your church, and if you still have time you can go somewhere else and be a blessing to them.

There are some people who leave their local assembly and take their tithe to the headquarters of their church, which is not where they attend every time. They fund projects at the headquarters and contribute immensely to build the headquarters while their local assembly, where they are fed constantly, is neglected. Some people even give big prophets offering to a visiting pastor from the headquarters or a popular man of God who was invited to come and preach, yet they never give a dollar to the pastor who has been preaching and praying every day for them. I have also seen people who go to another church when their own church has need of them. Your church has a convention and another church invites you to their concert at the same time, and because you hear that a big pastor is going to preach there, you leave your own to attend another when you were needed to be a part of your event. Your resources should be used primarily to service your church; every other place is secondary. Your energy and abilities should be used to serve in your primary place of assignment, for that is where the blessing will be delivered.

Your Home

Your home is another place of service. The Scripture says in 1 Timothy 5:8:

> But if any provides not for his own, and especially for those of his own house, he hath denied the faith, and is worst than an infidel.

Charity begins at home. Your family is your primary place of responsibility after God. You have a duty to service your family and make everything okay before you start looking outside. This is the number one cause of problems in many marriages today, especially in some cultures. As a husband, you have a duty to your wife first and if you have children, they are first before your parents. It is good to take care of your parents, but that should come after you have taken care of your immediate family first.

You can't deny your wife her request and be busy lavishing gifts to your mother and father. You can't leave your wife and children hungry and display your wealth outside by sponsoring projects in church so that people will respect you and the church can give you position; that is absolute nonsense. God will never accept that from your hand so it is a waste. Your money should first be used to settle those in your house before anyone can benefit from it. Remember your primary place of service is to those of your household. This applies to a woman also if she is the breadwinner. Don't despise your husband and keep him hungry because he has no job and be wearing fancy clothes and be giving fat checks in church to show that you are a woman of substance; instead, help your husband stand on his feet, and your family will go places.

After you have removed your tithe, which is God's portion, from your wage, use the remaining to take care of your home. Some people will leave their immediate family and attend to distant relations and parents while their spouse and children are in need. It is not what you do in church that shows you serve but what you do in your home. Your service begins at home because that is where God has placed you, and whatever you do there eventually affects the world. If the home is good, the community will be good and eventually the world. Your service starts at home.

Place of Work

Your place of work is another place of service. If you take your job as though you are working for God, he will bless you. Don't go to work and treat people badly or work as though you are being forced to do it. There are some people who own shops or business, but the manner in which they treat their customers is appalling; they quarrel with everyone and sometimes I ask them if they are forced to do the business. Your place of work is where you can serve God because everyone is looking just as God is watching you.

SERVICE IS A CHOICE

JOSHUA 24: 15-16

And if it seems evil unto you to serve the LORD, **choose** you this day whom ye will serve; whether the gods which your fathers served that were on the other side of the flood, or the gods of the Amorites, in whose land ye dwell: **but as for me and my house, we will serve the LORD.**

Service is a choice that only you make.

Nobody is ever coerced to serve God; it is a choice that you make.

JOSHUA 24: 15-16

And if it seems evil unto you to serve the LORD, **choose** you this day whom ye will serve; whether the gods which your fathers served

> that were on the other side of the flood, or the gods of the Amorites, in whose land ye dwell: **but as for me and my house, we will serve the LORD.**

You can make a choice to serve God or you can choose not to. Everything that happens in our life depends largely on the choices that we make. When God created man, he put in man a will; this will makes man not to be a robot or a puppet in the hand of God. Man has a choice to do whatever he wants without any interference from God. That is why you see people going to the soccer field on Sunday morning when you are going to church; you can't stop them because they have made a choice to play football while you made a choice to go to church.

When you have made a choice to serve God, you need empowerment to be able to serve. It is one thing to choose to serve and another thing to be able to serve. I remember how many times some people told me that God has placed the desire in their hearts to join the sanctuary unit of the church and up till this moment I haven't seen any of them. This means that God has placed in their hearts the desire to serve, and they sincerely want to serve, but the empowerment to serve is not there. It is the spirit of servanthood that helps us render service to God. This spirit boosts our capacity and empowers us even when we feel like giving up. You can make a choice to serve, but you need empowerment. Just like you make a choice to study a particular course in school or go a particular spot for a vacation, you can make a choice to serve God. If you choose not to serve him, no one would blame you, and when you see others giving testimonies of God's goodness in their lives, you don't have to feel bad because it was your choice not to serve.

As Joshua pointed out to the children of Israel to make a choice of service, I am asking you today to make a choice to serve if you haven't done so. The cheapest way to a breakthrough in life is for you to serve God. I can say this with confidence because am a living witness. A choice to serve God is a choice to advancement in life. There are people who used to serve God, but at the very point of their breakthrough, they back out. Why? Because they made a choice not to continue and the blessing stayed away from them.

Make a choice today to serve him. The power is in your hands to serve God and when you have decided, God will empower you to do your part through the empowerment of the spirit of servanthood. As a parent, when you have made a choice to serve God, encourage your children to do the same so they can plant a seed for their future. It should not be only you but you and your household. A choice to serve God means that on Sunday you don't leave for church while your children stay home. Don't leave them behind; take them along with you and they will grow to make you proud. Train them to serve God and when they are old, they will not depart from it. God was proud of Abraham and he made a statement in Scripture that means your choice should not be for yourself but for your entire family.

GENESIS 18:19

> For I know him, that he will
> command his children
> and his household after him,
> and they shall keep
> the way of the LORD, to do
> justice and judgment;
> that the LORD may bring upon
> Abraham that which
> he hath spoken of him.

When you have made a choice to serve God, make sure that your entire family walks in that choice so that the blessing of God may be upon your house. Don't choose to serve while the rest are wayward, doing what they like and sometimes serving other Gods right under your roof when you don't have any idea, and even when you do, you say, "They will change when they grow up." Make a choice to serve God because he deserves your service. He has kept you alive and taken care of you, he didn't allow the enemy to consume you, and what can you give in return except to render service to him. May the Lord give you understanding.

EYE SERVICE

EPHESIANS 6:6-7

Not with **eye service**, as
menpleasers; but as the
servants of Christ, doing
the will of God from the heart;
With goodwill doing service,
as to the Lord and not to men.

There is so much eye service going on in the church today. People pretend to serve, but they are actually not serving God but deceiving themselves. You are doing eye service when you only serve for people to see or for man's approval. In Ephesians 6:6-7 the Bible says,

Not with **eye service**, as
menpleasers; but as the
servants of Christ, doing
the will of God from the heart;
With goodwill doing service,
as to the Lord and not to men.

The spirit of servanthood will enable you to serve God without looking for man's approval. I have never seen a child who does house chores to gain approval from their parents. When I was a kid, it was my responsibility to wake up in the morning and sweep the house and when I finished sweeping, I would check the drum and see if there was water and if there was none, I would go and fetch water so my parents could take their bath before I left for school. Most times I was late to school because of the things I had to do before leaving the house. I never did my house chores so my parents would see, nor did I do them to get favor; it was my responsibility.

If we do the work of God the way children do their responsibilities at home for their parents, then we will be far from eyes service. Unfortunately, the case is different in the house of God; people do all kinds of things just to get commendations. They do things to please people, not because they truly want to do those things. When the time comes for the church to ordain people by giving titles, that is when people start going to church, and after the ordination you don't see them again, the reason being that either they have gotten the title they wanted or they were not ordained and so you don't see them in the church anymore.

You are doing eye service when all that is in your heart is for the church to see and give you position.

Many people go to church not because they love God or truly want to be in church but because they have a title to defend. Some even give because they have a title in church and it will look bad if they don't give. I have seen a situation where people run around or look busy in church because the general overseer of their church is around and when he leaves, you don't see them anymore. Some, because they want a position, you see them in every service and activity in church and as soon as they get what they want, you don't see them anymore.

The spirit of servanthood will empower you to serve without eye service. It will enable you to serve without looking for any reward in return. Let us understand here that any eye service will never be rewarded by God, for he is not a respecter of man. If you are doing eye service in God's house, you are only deceiving yourself and eventually one day there will be a distinction between those who served God sincerely and those who were doing eye service.

Here is some of the eye service we see in church today.

If you have a beautiful car and you use it to carry the pastor but refuse to carry that sister or brother whom you think has nothing, you are doing eye service.

You go to church only when you know the general overseer of your church is around. This is eye service.

Because you sit near a beautiful lady in church, you bring out lots of money to put in the offering basket so she can see that you have money. You are doing eye service.

You go to church just to show a new dress you bought. You are doing eye service.

If you buy things for the pastor and refuse to meet the needs of your loved ones, you are doing eye service.

You pray loud in church and even speak in tongues so that everyone can see how holy you are, yet you treat people badly outside the church environment; you are doing eye service.

Because your church is about to ordain new ministers, that is when you start going to every activity early and begin to smile with those you never greet or regard as anything; you are doing eye service.

The Scriptures say in Mathew 5:16:

> Let your light so shine before men, that they may see your good works, and glorify your father which is in heaven.

It is your light that must shine, not you telling people that you are shining. When you are baptized with the spirit of servanthood, you will not need to broadcast what you do but people will notice it. It is your light that will shine through the spirit of servanthood at work in you, and then people will see the good things that you have been doing and they will glorify God and not you.

As a member of the sanctuary unit, at a particular branch of my church where I was at the time, I was always in the bathroom and my duties were to flush the toilet and clean it as people were using it. I never knew that someone was watching me. One day, a young man came to join the unit and when he was asked why, he said that he always saw me flushing the toilet without looking at anybody; then he said in his heart, "If this man can do it, I can do it also." He saw me as someone who should not be doing that but because I did it, he too could do it. It is your light that will always shine to show your good work.

If only people will learn to serve God sincerely from their hearts, we can never imagine the blessings that will come. Eye service destroys because it is deceptive. The devil does not fear your title; if you like, be an archbishop, but if you are not a servant, you are wasting your time. Eye service is the weapon the devil is using to destroy the Church of Jesus today. Many people are just busy doing eye service and expect to be blessed. The reason many are in the church today and do not experience any blessing is because all that they have been doing in the church has not been recorded in heaven because they are busy pleasing people. The day we begin to serve sincerely is when we begin to experience God's blessings. God does not call us to serve him in vain, according to Isaiah 45:19.

MOTHER OF ALL SERVICE

MARK 16:15

And he said unto them, Go ye into all the all the world, and preach the gospel to every creature.

Soul winning is the mother of all service. According to the opening Scripture of this chapter, we have a divine mandate to preach the word to everyone. And for you to preach the gospel to everyone, you must reach out to them. There are so many Christians who do not fulfill this mandate. When you are saved, it is your duty to make sure others are saved too. There is no service in the kingdom that is comparable to soul winning. No matter how much you give in terms of finances to move the kingdom forward, or the good things you do in the church as in service, it can never be compared to one soul that you bring to church and is established in the faith. The Scripture says that nothing in this world can be compared to the soul of a man.

MARK 8:37

Or what shall a man give
in exchange for his soul?

And it is also recorded in the Scripture of truth that there is joy in the heaven over one sinner that repents.

LUKE 15:7

I say unto you, that likewise
joy shall be in heaven over one
sinner that repenteth...

That means angels in heaven throw a party when there is a new convert. There is no such joy in heaven when you give a billion dollars for a crusade, but when you finally lead one sinner to Christ, you have sparked joy in heaven and you can imagine God the father smiling as the angels party. Preaching the gospel to the lost and bringing them the faith is our primary task as Christians and it is the mother of all service.

I believe that reaching out to the lost with all your heart, whether privately or collectively, is the best activity in which you can engage yourself in the body of Christ. Every day we are presented with the opportunity of speaking to people, and if we catch the moment, we might be saving someone who was heading to hell.

I had the privilege of covering a surprise bridal shower for one of the sisters in our church and when it was time for people to talk about the bride, three ladies gave testimonies that it was the bride who brought them to church. I was amazed even as one of them said she saw her on a bus and spoke to her and now those ladies are grounded in the church and blazing the trail for Jesus.

What a joy and what rewards await that daughter of God. People will forget what you gave in church and they may even forget the services you rendered, but a sinner you bring to Jesus will never forget that you brought him or her. I was brought to Jesus by my mother and I gave my life to Jesus at the age of eleven, even though I later left and began to be involved in the world and going so deep, but the seed had been planted and at the appointed time, it germinated and I am back, planted and serving and telling everyone who cares to hear that Jesus is the Lord and that he loves everyone to the point of dying on the cross.

You are a wise man if you are in the business of winning souls for Jesus.

PROVERB 11:30

...and he that winneth souls is wise.

DANIEL 12:3

And they that be wise shall shine
as the brightness of the firmament;
and they that turn many to righteousness
as the stars for ever and ever.

God places emphasis in soul winning. He says that if you win a soul for him then you are a wise man and because of that wisdom, you shall reign in this life and in the life to come. We must rise up in this end time and begin to seek for the lost souls and bring them to Jesus. If you are born again, you must make sure no one in your family continues in sin but must be brought to light. In soul winning, there are those who go out to the field (I call these people "foot soldiers") and there are those who go out on their knees. They commit themselves to praying for the lost souls in their neighborhood, family, or community. Because of one limitation or the other, they decided to win souls on their knees. The reason why you go out and talk to people and they follow you may not be because you know how to preach, but because someone is somewhere on the knees praying for them and you just go out and it's easy to catch them for Jesus.

Soul winning is the heartbeat of God because he wants everyone to repent; it is not his will that anyone should perish.

2 PETER 3:9

> The Lord is not slack concerning his promise, as some men count slackness; but is longsuffering to us-ward, not willing that any should perish, but that all should come to repentance.

Hellfire was not made for man but for the devil, and so God does not want man whom he created in his likeness to suffer the punishment meant for the devil and demons. That is why he has commanded us to go out and preach to everyone so they can repent and make heaven. The spirit of servanthood is what enables us to pursue soul winning because it cannot be done in the arm of the flesh. You cannot wake up suddenly and say, "I want to win souls." No, you will not be able to do it effectively and get results; you need empowerment and direction. If you jump on the boat with a hook and say you are going fishing, you may return empty because you need to understand how fishing works. If you go out on the first day and no soul returns with you or everyone you stop to speak to does not answer you, you will be discouraged.

There was a time I went out with some tracks to share and with the mind of talking to anyone who would give me their time. I started handing out the tracks and no one collected from me to a point that I was so discouraged that I put the tracks in my bag and refused to share them. You may be frustrated if no one answers you so you need to be empowered so that no matter how many people refuse you, you will still go ahead until you get the one that God has ordained for salvation and you see that person respond quickly.

Soul winning brings more blessings than any kingdom service. If you are looking for a job and can't get any, switch to soul winning and jobs will start looking for you. If you want a life partner and you have prayed enough, go out to win souls and your spouse will come running after you. You may even meet your spouse in the course of evangelism; I have heard such testimonies many times. Whatever you want from God, and you have prayed and fasted and it seems not to come, join the evangelism unit and engage it with all your heart; in the course of it, God will be meeting those needs accordingly, with speed. In this age of social media, it is the best platform to reach out to people and tell them about Jesus.

Social media is very effective and it influences people's lives more than we can imagine. I got to know this when once I posted on my Facebook wall that "if you want to marry, make sure your spouse is born again, otherwise you will be going into what you will regret forever and the devil will be your father-in-law." A few hours later, a young man sent me a message saying, "Thank you, sir, for that post. I have a wedding coming up in few weeks but when I read your post I pondered on it and decided to cancel the wedding because the message touched me and saved me from making a mistake." You can preach the gospel through your social media and when we get to heaven, you will be amazed at how many lives you saved.

I used my BlackBerry messenger to preach to someone I used to know years back but had not seen for a long while; she accepted Jesus, went to church according to my instruction, got baptized, joined the Bible training program of the church, and eventually became a secretary of a home cell fellowship. She posted her baptism certificate and others for me to see. That is the power of social media. We have no excuse not to talk to people about Jesus whether far or near. The time you spend chatting on Facebook and Twitter you could have chatted someone out of the waters of sin into the glorious liberty of Christ. God can pay you anything for the soul of one person you bring to Jesus.

HUMAN WORSHIP

ISAIAH 29:13

Wherefore the Lord said, Forasmuch as this people draw near me with their mouth, and with their lips do honor me, but have removed their heart far from me, and their fear toward me is taught by the precept of men.

MATHEW 15:8-9

This people draweth nigh unto me with their mouth, and honor me with their lips; but their heart is far from me. But in vain they do worship me, teaching for doctrines the commandments of men.

Our opening Scripture for this chapter tells us exactly what is going on in the church today. Human worship can easily be seen in Christian denominations, people serving men instead of serving God. They call the people they worship "my father in the Lord" yet they do not reflect the unction upon those they worship. Instead of them worshipping the God of the man, they worship the man. This is a gross error.

It is not talking too much about the person you follow; it is about reflecting that person. If who you follow is your father in the Lord, reproduce the unction on that person; otherwise, it will be a "charismatic title of convenience" according to Bishop David Oyedepo. The apostles followed Jesus and they reflected Jesus by doing miracles (which were the trademarks of Jesus). They did not talk much about him for people to listen to them; they simply duplicated him to the point that they were given the name "Christians."

Some people go as far as making their hair look like that of the pastor they follow. Some even talk like the pastor and dress like him but lack the power the man operates with. If you dress, talk, and fashion yourself like the pastor you follow but do not manifest the power, you are just busy doing human worship. You are not supposed to serve man but God. There are some members who prostrate to greet their pastors, while some pastors demand that you greet them with two hands, prostrate, or kneel down. Human worship is not service and does not show that you are a true servant. Some who prostrate to greet can't even wait for the man of God to leave before they start talking against him.

Elisha served Prophet Elijah and even called him "my father," but he was a true servant who reflected his master, duplicating the anointing of his master in a double portion.

2 KING 3:11-12

> But Jehoshaphat said, is there not
> here a prophet of the Lord, that we
> may inquire of the Lord by him?
> And one of the king of Israel's
> servants answered and said, Here
> is Elisha the son of Shaphat, which
> poured water on the hands of Elijah.

The man reflected his master in so much that everyone knew about him and all his mockers had to worship him. If you serve God and follow the man he has set over you sincerely, soon people will begin to see you function as your master. Let us stop worshipping man thinking we are worshipping God. Let all worship and service be directed to God so that we can receive blessings meant for us. The reason we need empowerment of the spirit of servanthood is to help us serve God and not man. The spirit cannot come upon you and you still render service to man; it will be to God. If we crave the spirit of servanthood the way we crave titles and position in church, we will be far from human worship, and our service will be effective and directed to God.

REPUTATION CONSCIOUSNESS

PHILIPPIANS 2:5-9

Let this mind be in you, which also was in Christ Jesus: Who, being in the form of God, thought it not robbery to be equal with God: But made himself of **no reputation**, and took upon him the form of a servant, and was made in the likeness of men: And being found in fashion as a man, he humbled himself, and became obedient unto death, even the death of the cross. Wherefore God also hath highly exalted him, and given him a name which is above every name.

There is too much reputation consciousness in church today.

I was in the church one day for fellowship and a man walked in. He was dressed like a pastor; I saw him but didn't pay much attention to him. The usher gave him a seat at the back and he started demanding to speak with the senior pastor. The service was going on and the usher told him that was not possible until after the service. The man began to get upset and shouted at the usher that he didn't know the protocol. He mentioned his title and almost interrupted the service. I was called but before I could handle the situation he left out of anger. This among others shows that people simply want to be recognized. I have received notes from people that I should give to the leadership of the church to honor their presence in a church service. What is wrong with going to church and sitting quietly, enjoying the service and also seeing things in a different perspective without sitting on the altar?

The reason people want recognition in church is because they are not servants. They are rulers of Gentiles; they want the best place in functions and want everyone to know they are there. They want to sit on the altar every time. They fight to be given prayer points or other duties that will make them looked upon as deacons, pastors, or elders, and if you don't give them they get angry. Some even give to maintain their status in church, not because they love God. People just want to be seen; they want recognition.

They want you to acknowledge them and greet them by their title any time you see them.

You cannot have the spirit of servanthood and be reputation-conscious. Jesus Christ humbled himself and he was elevated to sit at the right hand of Majesty on high. Jesus made himself of no reputation; in fact, after healing some people, he commanded them not to tell people and at other times when he cast out demons and they started talking, he silenced them so they would not say who he truly is. But if you heal one person, you broadcast it so people will know you have the anointing. If you give money to the church for a particular project, you want your name announced so that others will know you did it. This is not the way a servant should behave. You need the spirit of servanthood. Do not go around telling people what you have done for God; otherwise, you will be seeking for reputation. Let us follow the footsteps of Jesus by humbling ourselves so that we can be raised up. Jesus came as God yet did not seek to be heard.

The spirit of servanthood made him seek to fulfill the mission God gave to him and not to raise himself up for the world to see and know that he is the son of God. See where that has taken him to today. As a true servant, you don't have to seek to be heard; your title means nothing if you use it to boast and make people see you instead of Christ. If you are reputation-conscious, you are not a servant. As a servant, you must not seek to be heard, according to our opening Scripture, but must be humble and ready to serve. Fighting and doing all kinds of things just to be ordained in church is reputation consciousness.

PRIDE, THE BANE OF SERVANTHOOD

ISAIAH 42:1-4

Behold my servant, whom I uphold;
mine elect, in whom my soul delighted;
I have put my spirit upon him: he shall
bring forth judgment to the Gentiles.
He shall not cry, **nor lift up**...

JAMES 4:6

But he giveth more grace. Wherefore
he saith, God resisteth the proud,
but giveth grace unto the humble.

Pride is what ruins our service to God. This is why we need to be baptized with the spirit of servanthood, so we can be saved from pride. No matter how far you have gone in ministry as a pastor or how involved you are in the things of God, you can be brought low because of pride. Many people have lost out in their blessings because of pride. Pride is a serious sin because you may not even know you are proud or serving with pride. It is also the first sin ever recorded and it emanated from someone who was entrusted with a position of authority and that triggered pride in him. Our chapter Scripture says that God resists the proud. Whatever you do that is with pride makes God push you away.

There is a saying that "if you want to know the true character of a man, give him power." This saying is true because you may never tell the true nature of a man until you entrust him to a position of authority and you see him manifest in a way you never thought possible. Some people become so proud that you cannot even talk to them because they are now ordained as a pastor, deacon, or elder. Some pastors begin to raise their shoulders because they are counting a thousand members in their church. That is why God will not raise them above that level, and soon you see the members start leaving.

A simple promotion in the office or increase in wage will make some people unapproachable. One day in my local assembly, there was a meeting concerning an issue. Someone tried to raise a point, and he was immediately shut down by one of the pastors, who said, "When pastors are talking, you don't talk." This is pride. If he were humble, he would have heard that brother out and maybe he would have had the answer to that issue because God can speak through anybody.

The story of Balaam and the donkey is a clear example that God can speak to anyone, no matter how highly or lowly placed, through an unlikely source. Sometimes when the people at the top are too proud and God really wants to convey his message, he can use a janitor.

There is too much pride going on in the body of Christ that makes one ask, "Are we really serving the master?" Some people, because of position, you can't even talk to them. Some use that position to oppress others and do all manner of disgusting things in the name of title.

Pride goes before a fall. Watch anyone who walks in pride; they will not last long because pride is a destroyer. When you see yourself too much, God will bring you low. As a leader, you must be humble because that is the only way you can know what to do. Pride has never taken anyone far; it always leaves the proud stranded on the highway of life. When you humble yourself, God will lift you up. Your anointing will be ruined if you are proud. It takes humility to stay at the top. When God has elevated you, see that as an opportunity to serve him and humble yourself so that the promotion can be sustained.

Do not look down on people because you have been promoted or given a particular title or leadership role because that is going to be your downfall. There was a king in the Bible whom God destroyed because of pride. His name was Herod.

ACTS 12:21-23

> And upon a set day Herod, arrayed in royal apparel, sat upon his throne, and made an oration unto them. And the people gave a shout, saying, It is the voice of a god, and not of a man. And immediately the angel of the Lord smote him, because he gave not God the glory: and he was eaten of worms, and gave up the ghost.

God gave Herod a position of authority and because of that, pride entered his heart and he began to talk big. He did not give glory to God. The people around him saw the way he carried himself, and they helped in his downfall by proclaiming him as God; therefore, the judgment of God came upon him swiftly.

You see, when you are given a position of authority, you must acknowledge God and still humble yourself no matter how high you think you have climbed. Another thing is that you should be careful of those around you because some of them are sycophant. They can praise you to your downfall. There was a time someone who was invited to the fifty-thousand-capacity auditorium of Winners Chapel and he began to praise Bishop David Oyedepo for accomplishing such a great thing. Immediately Bishop David Oyedepo climbed the podium and began to sing:

> "All the glory must be to the
> Lord for he is worthy
> of our praise, no man on
> earth should give glory
> to himself, all the glory must be to the Lord."

The bishop acknowledged that God is the doer and without him he could not have accomplished that. He had to save himself from trouble. There are some people who would have sat down there and enjoyed the praise and before you knew it, pride would enter their hearts. Pride has destroyed many ministry and numerous services that people have rendered in the house of God. We must be careful to give praise to God.

THE PLACE OF OBEDIENCE

JOB 36:11

> If they obey and serve him, they
> shall spend their days in prosperity,
> and their years in pleasure.

Obedience is everything in kingdom service. If you are a true servant of God, you will obey him. Your response to the voice of God will depend largely on the spirit at work in you. There are many people God has spoken to and they refused to listen because what he said did not sound convenient to them. Little did they know that it was an instruction to their next level and so they keep struggling. Jesus said in John 10:27:

> My sheep hear my voice, and
> I know them, and they follow me.

There is no sheep that determines where it is to grass or where to get water. They follow the shepherd wherever he leads them. True servants of God will always obey God no matter how it sounds or looks. Unfortunately, today people find it difficult to obey God. They do not want to move outside their comfort zone. Whatever God says that is not comfortable to them will not be obeyed. If as a pastor, God asks you to leave a particular area and move to another, if you obey, you will see increase but if you remain because according to you, you do not want to lose members, then you are in for a downfall or stagnation. The church you pastor does not belong to you but to Jesus. You don't own it; you are only a physical overseer. The owner of the church is Jesus, according to Mathew 16:18:

> And I say unto thee, that thou art Peter, and upon this rock I will build my church; and the gates of hell shall not prevail against it.

That is why from time to time he will come out with plans to move his church forward but you thwart that move with lack of obedience. The above Scripture says Jesus will build his church, not the pastor or church board. Lack of obedience has stagnated many churches that would have exploded into global wonder. The same applies to our businesses and jobs. Going into ministry as a servant will make you yield to the leading of the Holy Spirit. He will take you through one step at a time and in the process train you for the big task ahead. But if you refuse to obey and want to start big then that ministry may not see the light of the day, as I have witnessed in many cases.

It is obedience that makes Living Faith Church Worldwide (aka Winners Chapel) a global phenomenon today. When God asked Bishop David Oyedepo, the founder, to move from the city to the forest, a place where no one wants to go, it seemed like utter madness, but his obedience has turned him into a global wonder. We should understand that God never leads any man backward and everything he does is absolute perfection. His leading may look backward, but it's a road to greatness. Maybe God wants to use you to display his power to the kingdom of darkness and your disobedience will frustrate that plan; do you know how that will make him feel? I tell people that where the headquarters of Winners Chapel, "Canaan land," is located now is proof of God's power over the kingdom of darkness. That location was the coven of witches, I think the most wicked witches in the world. It was a conglomerate of the powers of darkness. God wanted to displace them, and when he found a man of obedience, he was able to accomplish his purpose. In your business and career, you need to yield to the leading of the Holy Spirit, and if you do, you will become great. Obedience is very important in kingdom service, for to obey is better than sacrifice.

1 SAMUEL 15:22

> And Samuel said, Hath the LORD as great delight in burnt offerings and sacrifices, as in obeying the voice of the LORD? Behold to obey is better than sacrifice, and to hearken than the fat of rams.

You may be serving God passionately and he decides to change your story by asking you to give him your one week's or one month's salary depending on where you are in the world and the method of wage payment. Instead of obeying, you keep praying, serving, and declaring. My friend, you may not see a change of level because the instruction has been given, but you don't want to follow. God works in mysterious ways. Maybe there is a yoke in your family or lineage that must be broken and God, who is all-knowing, wants you to give something to break that yoke but your disobedience blocks that.

This world we are living in is more spiritual than physical. There are things your physical eyes cannot see and many of the afflictions of men can be overturned through a simple spiritual instruction which most times sounds stupid. Many Christians don't pay tithe and so they suffer lack, stagnation, and oppression from the wicked one. The devourer has a field day in their lives. The instruction is to pay your tithe but they refuse and decide to fast. I bet you may die on the altar of fasting if you don't obey that simple instruction of paying your tithe. For you to experience peace in your marriage, the Bible says for husbands to love their wives and for the wives submit themselves. If you obey this Scripture, you will not only experience peace but a lasting union, but many people don't want to obey this and so they end up seeking divorce.

One day God asked me to give him something that would cost me. I looked around and the only thing I had was my laptop, which was the most and only valuable thing in my life. I thought it was a joke; how can God ask me to give the only thing that remained after I had lost everything and the laptop is the only thing that contained information I could use to start all over again? After a few days, I went to church for a weekly program and the pastor said, "There is someone here that God has asked to give him something, and this week is the last and if you don't obey, you are to blame." As he said that, I knew that it was me he was talking about and my spirit was disturbed. This was a Wednesday, and on Saturday I went for house fellowship and as we concluded the closing prayer, a sister in the fellowship asked the cell leader, "Please, do you know where in the Bible it says 'Gather my saints together unto me; those that have made a covenant with me by sacrifice'?" (Psalm 50:5.) I said, not again, this is God giving me a final warning, and, the next day being Sunday, I had to make sure I gave him the laptop in the offering basket, after all efforts to sell it and give the cash proved impossible. It was after giving the laptop that I was at peace and was able to sleep well; since then, the heavens opened and I am on a journey to greatness.

When God asks you to do something, it is so he can bless you, not because he needs what he asked you to give. There is a woman who was looking for the fruit of the womb, and she heard a man of God preach about kingdom service, asking people to join service units in church and serve. She obeyed and joined the sanctuary keepers to clean the toilet. Today that woman is a mother of children through simple obedience. In your place of service, whether in your service unit in church or workplace, you must learn to obey. Hebrew 13:17 says that we must obey those who have rule over us.

Obedience is very important and our chapter Scripture says that if you obey and serve, you shall spend your days in prosperity. You are guaranteed to prosper if you obey God and serve him.

Often, we spend too much energy praying for our needs when those needs could have been a workover if only we serve. I am a beneficiary of the blessing of service. I don't struggle like others; things just fall into place for me because I am committed to serving God. Since I caught this secret called kingdom service, I have been doing it as if my life depends on it, and I am a living testimony that God truly blesses those who serve him. If you obey and serve God, you too will spend your years in pleasure.

SERVICE: THE PATHWAY TO GREATNESS

PHILIPPIANS 2:5-9

Let this mind be in you, which was also in Christ Jesus: Who, being in the form of God, thought it not robbery to be equal with God: But made himself of no reputation, and took upon him the form of a servant, and was made in the likeness of men; And being found in fashion as a man, he humble himself, and became obedient unto death, even the death of the cross. Wherefore **God also hath highly exalted him**, and given him a name which is above every name.

There is no true servant of God who is not on his or her way to greatness, no matter how he or she may look today. Jesus is an example of how the spirit of servanthood can take you to high places in life, according to the anchor Scripture of this chapter. The Bible says that God hath highly exalted him after he humbles himself to serve. Now this man was with God in heaven before he came to earth. He did not puff up and say I am the son of God; instead, he humbled himself and decided to serve despite his position as a divinity. The reason many of us are not elevated in life is because we lay too much emphasis on our academic prowess and success in our field of endeavor instead of humbling ourselves so we can be raised to the highest of heights.

We are going to look at a few other people in Scriptures who served God and were made great. These individuals showed exceptional qualities of service and God promoted them. If we follow in their footsteps, we will soon also be promoted.

Abraham

Abraham was a true servant who was ready to obey God to the letter. In Genesis chapter 12, we saw how God called Abraham to leave his father's house to a place where he would show him. Now this is a very difficult instruction because someone you never met and can't even see told you to leave where you live and go to where you don't know. How would that sound? But Abraham obeyed and everything God asked him to he did and he served God faithfully until he became his close confidant.

GENESIS 18:17

> And the Lord said, shall I hide
> from Abraham that thing which
> I do.

He served his way into the heart of God that the Almighty himself took him as a close confidant, and revealed to him his plans concerning wayward nations. In James 2:23, we see Abraham being referred to as the friend of God.

> And the Scripture was fulfilled which
> saith, Abraham believed God, and
> it was imputed unto him for
> righteousness: and he was called the
> friend of God.

Serving God brought greatness to Abraham, and not just ordinary greatness; he became the only human being that God called his friend. If you want to be great in life, the best way is to serve. The story of Abraham is a very humbling one because we see all that he passed through and the challenges he faced but he kept serving and eventually became a generational blessing and up till today many crave his blessings even as we sing in songs, "Abraham's blessings are mine."

Before I continue, I would like to let you know that serving God is not easy. That is why we need empowerment through the spirit. For the flesh can be weakened but it is the spirit that is quickened. Engaging yourself in service units can be very frustrating sometimes because it is in church that you find people who are vindictive, cruel, mean, and judgmental. They will try to slow you down and most times discourage you but if you keep going on, you will reap the fruit of that service.

GALATIANS 6:9

And let us not be weary in well doing: for in due season we shall reap, if we faint not.

MOSES

Moses is an example of a true servant. The Bible says that Moses was the meekest man that ever lived.

NUMBERS 12:3

Now the man Moses was very meek above all the men which were upon the face of the earth.

Meekness is an attribute of a servant and this means you are humble, teachable, and patient. You cannot serve God if you are not humble because it takes humility to listen to God and follow him. The amazing thing is that meekness is an attribute of a leader and we see that in Moses when he had to lead millions of Israelites alone out of Egypt into their promised land. Moses was great because of his service and God made him a god to Pharaoh and the Egyptians; he was untouchable until he brought Egypt to its knees. What greatness. His service made him the only human being that saw what God looks like, and God himself testified of him in Numbers 12:7-8:

> My servant Moses is not so, who
> is faithful in all my house. With
> him will I speak mouth to mouth,
> even apparently, and not in dark
> speeches; and the similitude of
> the Lord shall he behold: wherefore
> then were ye not afraid to speak
> against my servant Moses.

Up till today, Moses is still seen as the greatest man that ever worked the face of the earth. On the mount of transfiguration as recorded in Mathew 17:4, we see Moses as one of those that appeared to our Lord Jesus. That means even in the afterlife, he is still in a place of authority. That is what service can do; it certainly can make you great.

JOSHUA

Service is truly a pathway to greatness and we see that in the life of Joshua. Joshua was a young man who served Moses; he was always by his side ministering to him. He was Moses' personal assistant. When Moses goes up to the mountain, Joshua will be at the foot of the mountain waiting and when Moses goes into the camp, he will wait for him at the tabernacle.

EXODUS 33:11

> And the Lord spake unto Moses face to face, as a man speaketh unto his friend. And he turned again into the camp: but his servant Joshua, the son of Nun, a young man, departed not out of the tabernacle.

Joshua served God through Moses passionately and sincerely, but you may ask me, "How do you know it was God he was serving and not Moses?" The answer is in Colossians 3:23-24, and that is why after Moses, he took over and became Israel's leader and is still counted as one of the greatest.

If you are given the opportunity to serve under a man, serve him as though you are serving God. Do all that you are asked to do with humility and sincerity. It is not until you join a service group or ordain as a worker that you begin to serve God. If you work under a man, do your job as though God employed you. Go to work on time, take your job hours seriously, be creative, and make all necessary input to make sure the organization grows. Learn to pray for your boss and the establishment that you work for, ask for expansion and God's blessing upon it, and surprisingly, you may be taken from the bottom to be the head of that organization.

Some of us may have heard of the story of Bishop David Abioye of Winners Chapel. He said that God called him to serve Bishop Oyedepo, and Bishop Oyedepo sent him to preach and he obeyed. He served Bishop Oyedepo to the point people started calling him names like "Oyedepo's boy." That didn't get to him because he is a true servant, and now he is celebrated worldwide. There is nowhere that Oyedepo is mentioned that Abioye is not mentioned too. He became great through service to God through man. That is what Joshua did and he became great. You too will be great if you serve.

Samuel

Samuel started out as a little boy serving under Eli the priest of God in 1 Samuel 3. As a little boy whom his mother loaned unto God, he lived in the temple with Eli and his sons. He served God faithfully and never followed the evil ways of Eli's sons. One day God revealed his plans to him in a vision, destroyed Eli and his sons, and put Samuel in their stead. It was Samuel who anointed Saul the first King of Israel and later David. Samuel's greatness was predicated on service.

David

The story of David is an interesting one. This is a boy who was not regarded as anything in his family. When Samuel went to David's village to anoint a new king, he invited David's family, but David himself was not invited by the father or brothers to that event that would produce a king. This goes to show that no matter how people may look down on you, spit at you, and regard you as nothing, only the plan and purpose of God will be fulfilled in your life. David, who was not invited to meet with Samuel, was in the bush serving his father as though he was serving God. He was taking care of the sheep and surprisingly, it was at the place of service that greatness met him. Samuel said that no one would sit until David arrived.

THE SPIRIT OF SERVANTHOOD

1 SAMUEL 16:11

> And Samuel said unto Jesse, Are here all thy children? And he said, There remaineth yet the youngest, and, behold, he keepeth the sheep. And Samuel said unto Jesse, send and fetch him: **for we will not sit down until he come hither**.

I am sure David's brothers were green in the face out of envy when he was anointed as king. But that is how God works. There is always a reward for service, especially when you serve sincerely from your heart. The one who was rejected and regarded as nothing ended up becoming the greatest king Israel ever had and is still talked about today. David was an addicted servant of God. In the book of Act 13:22, God testifies of him:

> And when he had removed him, he raised up unto them David to be their king; to whom also he gave testimony, and said, I have found David the son of Jesse, a man after mine own heart, which shall fulfill all my will.

When David was anointed king, the Bible records that he still went back to keeping the sheep. I know

David's attitude of service pleased God that he called him his servant.

PSALM 89:20

> I have found **David my servant**; with
> my holy oil have I anointed him.

David the servant was David the anointed. He was a servant; therefore, despite his anointing as the next king of Israel, he still continued in his service to his father by keeping the sheep (1 Samuel 16:19 and 17:28). He did not allow his position to enter his head. He was a true servant. In church today, if you ordain some people as pastor or deacon, or give them a position of leadership, they will not serve again. David served his way into the very heart of God that he called him "a man after my heart." The Messiah came from David's lineage, and we are beneficiaries of that today, but it all came through a man who set his heart to serve God.

Solomon

Solomon's rise to greatness was as a result of him serving God with his resources. He never held anything back but was ready to give all to God at every opportunity he had. His story challenges everyone because most of us, when God blesses us, we cannot even give back to him even that which belongs to him, which is ten percent. Solomon, although he was David's son, could not have been the greatest and richest king in his time if he wasn't giving to God. His love-motivated giving made him great. He could have died ordinary as others who succeeded him but for the fact that he chose to serve God generously with God-given resources. God had to make him great.

1 KING 3:3-5

> And Solomon loved the Lord,
> walking in the statutes of David
> his father: only he sacrificed and
> burnt incense in high places. And
> the king went to Gibeon to sacrifice
> there; for that was the great high
> place: and a thousand burnt offerings
> did Solomon offer upon that altar.
> In Gibeon the Lord appeared to
> Solomon in a dream by night: and
> God said, Ask what I shall give thee.

You see, everything we have comes from God and without him we cannot amount to anything. It is not your certificates or intellect or connections that have placed you where you are now but the love and mercy of God, and until you realize that you may not rise above your present level. When you serve God with your resources, either by funding church projects or giving to the poor, God will make you great. Solomon's service to God through his giving distinguished him and made him the greatest in his time. I mean there was no one like Solomon on the earth in his time that matches his riches and wisdom, and it all came on the wings of kingdom service.

I KING 4:29-32

> And God gave Solomon wisdom and understanding exceeding much, and largeness of heart even as the sand that is on the seashore. And Solomon's wisdom excelled the wisdom of all the children of the east country and all the wisdom of Egypt. For he was wiser than all men; than Ethan the Ezrahite, and Heman, and Chalcol, and Darda, the son of Mahol: and his fame was in all nations round about. And he spake three thousand proverbs: and his songs were a thousand and five.

This man was great indeed just by serving God. You cannot serve God and not be great on the earth. I have not seen any true, sincere servant of God that is a nonentity on the earth; he may look like nothing today, but surely he or she will be great. If you do not have time to be involved in service groups in your church, why not do like Solomon and serve him with your resources and see God distinguish you on the earth.

DANIEL

Many people think that you can only serve God when you are a pastor or an ordained worker in the church. Having a position in the church does not make you a servant; it is service that makes you a servant. You can be a pastor and yet you are not a servant of God. You can have all the big titles in church, yet you are not God's servant. Daniel was not a pastor or deacon; he was a politician. Now, many Christians think that you can't be a politician and still serve God; this is not true because Daniel was a politician yet he was a servant of God. He served God so sincerely that even the king and everyone else knew he was God's servant. People who plotted to remove him from office even testified of his total commitment to kingdom service.

DANIEL 6:5

Then said these men, we shall not
find any occasion against this
Daniel, except we find it against
him concerning the law of his God.

These men who planned to bring Daniel down knew that this man was too committed to God, thus making it impossible for him to fall. When you serve God genuinely, people around you will know. You don't need to tell people you are God's servant; they will know if you are or not. They couldn't remove Daniel in any other way, so they attacked him based on his kingdom service. If you are God's servant and once a week you carry your Bible and leave the office in time to go to Bible class, people at your job will know you and those who are your enemies will one day want to use it against you. When they schedule overtime and you refuse to work, this will anger them and sometimes they may try to schedule you for a Sunday job and when you refuse to accept, they will know you are servant of God, and soon they will want to play on that to refuse you a promotion or want to sack you. The king of Babylon then knew that Daniel was a true servant of God.

DANIEL 6:20

> And when he came to the den, he cried with a lamentable voice unto Daniel: and the king spake and said unto Daniel, O Daniel, servant of the living God, is thy God whom thou servest continually, able to deliver thee from the lions?

The king knew Daniel to be God's servant, and he also knew that Daniel served God continually, so it was not a one-time thing or when it was convenient. This meant that in summer he was serving, and during winter he never gave excuses but was still a servant. This made the king believe that this man who served his God this way must not be allowed to die just like that. So being a politician or holding a highly placed position is no excuse not to serve. When you serve God, he will make you great at your job, business, or any field you may find yourself.

Elisha

In 2 Kings 3:11-12, a king came to look for a prophet so that he may inquire of God's word from him, and a man whom no one had regarded as anything was introduced as the prophet in the land.

> But Jehoshaphat said, is there not here a prophet of the Lord, that we may inquire of the Lord by him? And one of the king of Israel's servants answered and said, Here is Elisha the son of Shaphat, which poured water on the hands of Elijah. And Jehoshaphat said, The word of the Lord is with him. So the king of Israel and Jehoshaphat and the king of Edom went down to him.

Elisha's rise to prominence was through faithful service to his master, Elijah, who was a prophet, and when he was no more, the mantle of office fell on him that kings had to go down to seek his guidance. There is no way you will serve faithfully that you will not be promoted in life. If you read through the book of 2 Kings, you will see that Elisha did more miracles than Elijah. Kings will look for you if you serve just as they looked for Elisha; men of substance will look for you if you serve God sincerely and faithfully.

JOSEPH

This chapter would not be complete if we didn't talk about one of the most interesting characters in the Bible: Joseph. This man was a slave in Potiphar's house yet he did not allow his circumstances to rule over him. He served his master so well that he was made the head of all other servants. His master, Potiphar, committed everything he had to him because of his faithfulness.

GENESIS 39:4

> And Joseph found grace in his sight, and he served him: and he made him overseer over his house, and all that he had he put into his hand.

When the wife of Potiphar tried to seduce him, he did not take advantage of her because he felt that would be a betrayal and a sin against God, whom he was serving through Potiphar. When Joseph was eventually put in prison for a crime he did not commit, he served in prison to the point that the warden put him in charge of other prisoners.

GENESIS 39:22

And the keeper of the prison committed
to Joseph's hand all the prisoners that were
in the prison; and whatsoever they did there,
he was the doer of it.

In his place of service, Joseph was always excited and cheerful and before anyone knew what was happening, he became the first and only prime minister of ancient Egypt, as recorded in Genesis 41:40.

Thou shall be over my house, and
according unto thy word shall all
my people be ruled: only in the
throne will I be greater than thou.

Joseph's greatness came as a result of his faithfulness in service. Despite what people did to him, he didn't hold grudges; neither was he bitter. He easily forgave and moved on. If you look at the story of Joseph, you will notice that he was always put in charge of any place he served. Why? Because he was faithful and committed. He served his masters as though he was serving God and always ended up being in control. When you serve faithfully in your primary place of assignment as though you are doing it unto God, he will eventually reward you. No one needs to watch or see what you are doing, but God sees and he who sees in secret will always reward in the open.

MOMENT OF DECISION

ROMANS 8:30

Moreover whom he did predestinate, them he also called: and whom he called, them he also justified: and whom he justified, them he also glorified.

If you serve without being born again, you are only engaging in activities that carry no reward.

You cannot serve unless you are called to do so.

ROMANS 8:30

Moreover whom he did predestinate, them he also called: and whom he called, them he also justified: and whom he justified, them he also glorified.

And before you can be called to serve, you must first believe in who you are to serve. Therefore, the first step to service is to surrender your life to Jesus, and if you have not done so already and want to do it now, please pray this simple prayer from the depths of your heart.

> *Lord Jesus, I come to you. I know I am a sinner, and I believe you came and died for me that I might be saved. I accept you, Jesus, as my Lord and Savior. Thank you, Jesus, for forgiving me. Thank you for saving me. Now I know my sins are forgiven. I am saved. I am born again. I am a child of God, old things are passed away and behold all things are become new. In Jesus' name, Amen.*

You may ask me, "Am I born again now with that simple prayer?" Oh yes, that simple prayer you prayed from the sincerity of your heart has changed your identity. You are now a child of God. You see, God's ways are so simple that that is why many people don't take it seriously. For God uses the foolish things of this world to confound the wise (1 Corinthians 1:27).

Now that you are born again, please look for a Bible-believing church, where the word of God is taught without fear or favor, and attend. And if you don't know any, I recommend you join the Living Faith Church, aka Winners Chapel, and attend. Join any service unit and serve your way to greatness. God bless you. See you at the top.

HOW TO GET THE SPIRIT OF SERVANTHOOD

1 CORINTHIANS 12:31

But covet earnestly the best gifts: and yet shew I unto you a more excellent way.

God does not waste his gifts on people; neither will he force anyone to receive something from him. Every spiritual gift in the kingdom can only come to you if you want it. In this chapter, I will show you by the help of the Holy Spirit how you can tap into this awesome spirit that will make you serve your way to greatness.

1. Desire it.

The Scripture says in Psalm 37:4,

Delight thyself also in the Lord; and he shall give thee the **desires** of thine heart.

Before you can receive any gift of the Spirit, you must first desire it. If you delight yourself in God yet there is no desire in your heart, God may not be able to give you anything. To get the spirit of servanthood, the first thing is for you to desire it. If you don't desire it, you may not have it.

Before I was baptized with the Holy Spirit, I desired it and one day as I was coming back from cleaning the church, while walking on the road, I prayed a simple prayer: "Jesus, please baptize me afresh with your Spirit." That was it. I had greatly desired the baptism of the Holy Ghost with the evidence of speaking in tongues and so after praying that prayer, I went home and forgot about it. At 8 p.m. Ghana time, my friends whom I lived with asked me to follow them to a cafe and unlike me, I said no. As soon as they left, I started hearing voices inside my stomach talking; now I was on my phone browsing through Facebook. Suddenly the voices became louder and it was as if someone said to me, "Won't you join them?" And immediately I started speaking in tongues but was still lying down. The voice said to me again, "Are you going to lie down there?" And I jumped to my feet, blasting in tongues till 10 p.m. Ghana time.

That was how I was baptized in the Holy Spirit and I believe the spirit to serve came upon me since then. So I must have had a full package. I was baptized alone in my room without anyone praying for me, just by desiring it. When you have a desire in your heart, God will give it to you, especially when it has to do with the things of the spirit. Apostle Paul said in 1 Corinthians 12:31:

> But covet earnestly the best gifts:
> and yet shew I unto you a more
> excellent way.

Some translations say "desire earnestly" so you can desire the spirit of servanthood, which is the spirit that will make you go all out for God and the things of the kingdom. It is the spirit that will make you great on the earth.

2. Ask in prayer.

You cannot receive anything from God, except you ask in prayer. In James 4:2 the Bible says,

> …yet ye have not, because
> ye ask not.

You cannot have unless you ask, and you ask in prayer. If you want to be baptized with the spirit of servanthood, you must approach God in prayer. Ask Jesus to baptize you with this spirit so you can serve effectively. It is not until you are faced with challenges that you begin to pray. Praying to receive a spiritual gift to me is more important because it is what will establish you as a child of God. You may not need to pray for any need if you are spiritually grounded. If you are baptized with the spirit of servanthood, which makes you serve God sincerely and effectively, many things others are praying for will just be added to you without you asking for it. If you want to excel in life, pray for spiritual gifts. The word of God says in Philippians 4:6:

> Be careful for nothing; but in
> everything by prayer and supplication
> with thanksgiving let your request
> be made known unto God.

3. Believe you have received.

After you have a desire in your heart, go to God in prayer concerning that desire. The next, which I consider to be very crucial, is to believe that you have received what you asked in prayer. This is exercising faith in God.

MARK 11:24

> Therefore I say unto you, What
> things soever ye desire, when ye
> pray, believe that ye receive them,
> and ye shall have them.

It is not enough to desire and to pray; you must believe that you have received what you asked for. You cannot be baptized with the spirit of servanthood just by desiring it or by praying about it. Your desire and prayers must be accompanied by faith, for the Bible says without faith it is impossible to please God. So you must have faith that your request has been approved. When I prayed that simple prayer, I believed that God heard me and I was at peace. That same day my answer came. Till today, I still believe that was the most truthful, sincere yet simple prayer I ever prayed in my life, but that was not what brought the answer. The answer came because I believed God heard me. Every time you go to God in prayer, believe that you have received what you ask of him and it will be given to you.

4. Begin to serve.

Now that you desire and have asked in prayer and also believe that you have received the baptism of the spirit of servanthood, begin to serve. The proof of that spirit at work in you will be in your service to God. Don't wait until a voice from heaven declares that God has baptized you before you serve; don't expect to have a spectacular visitation from heaven like I did before you know the Spirit is at work in you. The manufacturer of a car will always prove the power of the engine of the car only when they drive it. They don't sit down and expect the engine to perform; the performance is putting it on the road. You desired, asked in prayer, and even believed that it has been given, and then you must serve. Wherever you find yourself to serve, do it as if it is God that personally asked you to do it. People may try to discourage you with their attitude. Don't mind them. Remember it is God you are serving and not man, and soon those who oppose or mock you will see you at the top still serving God.

BENEFITS OF KINGDOM SERVICE

EXODUS 23:25-26

And ye shall serve the Lord your God, and he shall bless thy bread and thy water; and I will take sickness away from the midst of thee. There shall nothing cast their young, nor be barren, in thy land: the number of thy days I will fulfill.

The anchor Scripture for this chapter reveals to us the comprehensive package for kingdom service which no corporation on earth can afford to give to their employees. There are many benefits that accrue to those who serve God and I will enumerate them here by the help of the Holy Spirit so you can see that God does not take it lightly when you engage in kingdom service. I always like to tell people about my experiences which, by the grace of God, I have got a few of them.

One day it was raining heavily and everywhere was flooded. The house in which I stayed was flooded; everything in that house floated on the water. I used to hear about that happening, and that day I experienced it myself. On that same day, I had a friend who was in the hospital so I decided to scoop out the water as much as I could, and when I was tired I went to the hospital to see my friend. The doctors said they needed some payment to be made so they could continue treatment or else they would stop treating her. I had no money on me and the house I stayed was flooded. Immediately, the church at which I was worshipping at the time came into my mind and I decided to go and take a look. When I finally got there, everywhere was flooded and the church was in a mess so I decided to forget about my friend in the hospital and my flooded house and started cleaning out the water in the church.

Soon after, someone I never expect called on the phone and asked me if I had any problems. I told her about my friend in the hospital and the amount of money involved, and she said I should come and get it. God visited me with divine favor when I decided to serve him. When you serve God, he will bless you. The first benefit of kingdom service here is

1. Blessings.

When you serve God, he will bless you. It is the blessings of the Lord that terminate struggles in life. It is the blessings of the Lord that make us rich. We all need blessings and we can get them cheaply through kingdom service. When you serve God, you attract his blessings upon your life and that of your family. The blessings of God can come upon the works of your hand and make you a celebrity. All the great men in the Scripture served God from nothing till they rose to prominence. The blessings of the Lord can distinguish you in your career and set you above all those that were before you. God says he will bless your bread and your water; this means you will not struggle to get anything, but they will come to you because you serve him.

We all know that blessing is the opposite of curse. Therefore, the blessing of the Lord upon you through your service to him can terminate every form of curse that may be upon you. Many people go through life under a curse and so they struggle till they die. But when you serve God, these curses can be broken. If you are under a curse or you notice that your family has been operating under a curse, you can terminate it by engaging in kingdom service.

2. Divine health.

Kingdom service can attract divine health. When you serve God, he takes sickness away from you. Before I started serving God in the sanctuary unit of my church, I used to be very sick. I was diagnosed with enteritis, severe kidney infection that almost led to renal failure. I was born with chronic malaria, which my mom said I got from my dad. I had a severe ulcer and typhoid coupled with serious heart pain. I was a very sick person. I took malaria drugs every month among other treatments, but they didn't work.

When I started cleaning the church, these pains were still severe but after a while I forgot completely about it. One day, after several months in service to God, I suddenly remembered that I had not taken drugs for sickness and I wasn't feeling sick anymore. Praise the Lord, I was healed, but I didn't know God took away my sicknesses while serving him. My testimony shows that serving God can terminate sicknesses and diseases. If you are sick, serve God and he will take it away from you.

There are many things we pray about that I think we aren't supposed to waste time praying about. I never prayed for God to heal me; I just engaged in kingdom service and got my healing. There are many testimonies of diverse healing that occurred in the course of serving God. No matter the kind of sickness afflicting you, no matter the doctor's report, God can take it away if only you engage in kingdom service. There is no human establishment on this earth that can take sickness away from you; the most they can do is give free medical care, but that is not a guarantee because you can die in the process. But if you work for God, he takes sickness away from you completely.

3. Fruitfulness.

Our opening Scripture says that *there shall nothing cast their young, nor be barren in thy land:* because you serve the Lord. You are not permitted to be barren as a servant of the Lord. You cannot serve God and not be fruitful. There is a testimony of a woman who had been barren for many years. She came into the church and heard the man of God preach about kingdom service and so she went and joined the sanctuary unit and she was asked to clean the toilets during the convention, and the next year she became pregnant. Many years of barrenness was terminated in her life because of kingdom service. Let me say this, if you have been serving and you are still barren, maybe you are not doing it right because the word of God is true. God can never lie. He says if you serve, you shall not be barren. When you serve God, you have to serve sincerely; that is why you need the spirit of servanthood to help you. Don't serve and complain, murmur, or hold a grudge against anyone. No matter what anyone has done to you, don't be bitter, just let go so that your service can be acceptable to God and his reward will reach you quick. If you are serving God sincerely and you desire the fruit of the womb, I decree that you receive it now in the name of Jesus.

4. Long life.

Another benefit of service is long life. In Exodus 23:26 God says,

> The number of thy days
> I will fulfill.

This means that you are not permitted to die young if you are serving God. You are destined to longevity of life as a kingdom steward. Let me ask you, if you employ someone and he serves you faithfully, will you let that person go? That is what God is saying: "Because you are in my service, I will continue to keep you alive so you can continue to serve me." God's genuine servants don't die young. They can only pass on to glory after they are done fulfilling their service to God. God will always satisfy his servants with long life. Many people would have died long ago if they had not been in God service. I would have died, but God has kept his word in Exodus 23:25-26 in my life. I am alive because I serve and God has been very merciful to me. If you are threatened by death, go and engage yourself in kingdom service and experience the mighty hand of deliverance from God. If you serve, you will live long.

5. Prosperity.

Every true servant of God is entitled to prosperity. In Job 36:11, the Scripture says,

> If they obey and serve him, they
> shall spend their days in prosperity
> and their years in pleasure.

As a true servant of God, life has to be pleasurable to you. You can't serve God sincerely and lack anything. True servants always flow in wealth. If you work for a rich man and he loves your service, he will shower you with good things without you having to ask for it. The same goes with God. You can't serve God and wallow in poverty, lack, and want. He says if you obey and serve him, you shall spend your days in prosperity. This means that every day and everything you do must be prosperous. As a servant of God, your business must be prosperous; your academic life must be prosperous. Your family must be prosperous. Anyone in the line of your business must not match up with you if you are a servant of God. People should find you at the top if you are serving the Almighty

God. Things will just fall in place for you if you serve God, you don't need to beg for them.

When I see people in church who claim to have joined the church for many years yet nothing is working for them, and they are in the same position without anything to show that they are serving God, I get embarrassed because I know when you come to Jesus, your life must change. You must have something to show the world that it is good on this side of Jesus, and this can come cheaply by kingdom service.

6. Divine wisdom.

Divine wisdom means impeccable insight. Knowing what to do at every point in time. God can endow you with divine wisdom if you serve him. In the book of Daniel 1:17 the Bible records that God gave Daniel and the three Hebrew boys wisdom.

> As for these four children, God
> gave them knowledge and skill
> in all learning and wisdom...

God can give you wisdom so you can reign in life as his servant. If you read the book of Daniel, you will see how wisdom distinguished Daniel and the three Hebrew boys. They rise to prominence because of wisdom. In your place of work, God can use wisdom to promote you. Now that you know that wisdom is one of the benefits of kingdom service, engage in serving God passionately and see his wisdom manifest in your life. Joseph was another young man who enjoyed divine wisdom through kingdom service. In fact, in the whole of Egypt, there was no one that could compare to him in insight, so much so the king had to shift from the throne for him to rule.

GENESIS 41:38-39

And Pharaoh said unto his servants,
Can we find such a one as this is, a
man in whom the Spirit of God is?
And Pharaoh said unto Joseph,
forasmuch as God hath shewed thee
all this, there is none so discreet
and wise as thou art:

Wisdom distinguished Joseph and we know he was a faithful servant of God. The world has trade secrets but you can operate the wisdom which God can give to you to set you apart in that area of business only if you serve him. So many Christians today claim to be too busy for God. Any small promotion at work, you won't see them in church anymore. If they venture into a business, it becomes very difficult for them to serve God. Oh, if only they know their breakthrough lies in serving God. No matter what you do, if you don't allow it to hinder you from serving God, soon the world will celebrate you.

I have reached a point in my life that I can't take any job that will stop me from serving God. Anything that will hinder me from rendering quality service to God, count me out of it. I know where I came from and I know how it used to be. When God came into the scene, everything changed. Many people think I am stupid not to accept to work on some days because those days are my service days, but what they do not understand is that I would not even be alive if not for God. People complain about not having time even for midweek service because of their job and I ask, if God did not give you that job what you would do. God can give you wisdom to do something that will change your life and that of the world if only you are committed to serving him.

7. Divine connection.

If you are single and you want to marry, join a service unit in your church. Many people have been connected to their life partner just by belonging to a service unit in the church. Like I said earlier, God will always meet you at your place of assignment. You can't be single looking to get married and you go to church, sit through the service, and as soon as church is over, you are on your way home. You may not find what you are looking for easily like that. Get committed to a service group and your spouse may just be there waiting for you.

If you are looking for a job, join a service unit. Get involved in your church activities and you never know what you will get out of it. There is a testimony of a brother in my church who had been jobless for years after graduating from college. One day as he was doing his ushering service in my local church, a senior staff member of an oil company came in. He ushered the woman to her seat all smiles. The lady asked him if he had a job and he said no. She gave him a complimentary card and asked him to see her the next day in her office. That was it. He was given a job in an oil company and the next Sunday he testified. God can connect you with your dreams and desires if you position yourself to serve him.

There is another testimony of a sister in my church who was single and looking to get married. She joined the evangelism unit and engaged in it passionately. One day as they went out to evangelize, she preached to a man, brought the man to church, and he gave his life to Jesus. A few days later the man proposed to her and they are happily married now. You cannot serve God and go empty-handed.

8. Divine strength.

Divine strength is one of the benefits of kingdom service. In Psalm 105:37 the Scripture says,

> He brought them forth also with
> silver and with gold: **and there was not
> one feeble person among their tribe.**

And we remember in Genesis 9:1 God told Pharaoh to let his people go so they may serve him:

> Then the Lord said unto Moses, go
> in unto Pharoah, and tell him, Thus
> saith the Lord God of the Hebrews,
> let my people go that they may serve me.

When you have chosen to serve God and you do so with commitment, God is under obligation to keep you strong and energetic just as he did for the children of Israel. There is a testimony of a brother who was diagnosed with cancer and was told by the doctor that he would live for only a few months. He came and joined the crowd-control unit of our church and in the crowd control you have to stand all through the service. This man served for many months, even past the time the doctors had given him to live. This is what we call divine strength. You can't serve God and be feeble. No matter the doctor's report, if you engage in kingdom service, those who gave you a time limit will have to join you to serve God because of what they will see God do in your life. Divine strength is the portion of God's servants. No matter how old you are, no one will need to carry you about if you are serving God. No one will have to feed you or babysit you at seventy or eighty years if you are God's servant. Moses was a hundred and twenty and was still strong.

DEUTERONOMY 34:7

> And Moses was an hundred and twenty years old when he died: his eyes was not dim, nor his natural force abated.

The man Moses was strong till he died. He didn't need to be carried about even at that age. Divine strength is your portion if you serve God.

The prophet Elijah is another character that exhibited divine strength in the Scripture. Let's look at 1 Kings 18:46:

> And the hand of the Lord was on Elijah; and he girded up his loins, and ran before Ahab to the entrance of Jezreel.

Elijah, though an old man, is recorded in the Scripture to have run faster than a chariot. Chariots in those days were being driven by horses and you know horses are fast, but for an old man to outrun a horse-driven chariot then it must have been divine strength. Elijah was God's servant and at that time, he thought he was the only one serving God in Israel. So if you are a true and committed servant of God, divine strength will become your portion.

9. Protection.

When you serve God, he will protect you so you can continue to serve him. No witches can harm you if you serve God. There is a hedge round about every servant of God so that nothing can come to harm them. In Job 1:10 we see Satan complain about Job being divinely protected by God.

> Hast not thou made an hedge about him, and about his house, and about all that he had on every side? Thou has blessed the work of his hands, and his substance is increased in the land.

God protects those who serve him; he protects the works of your hands from being destroyed by the enemy. He puts a hedge round about your house and your children; that is why afflictions and plagues don't come near them. There is evil in the land and afflictions from hell are being poured upon the sons of men, but when you serve God, this evil can't come near your family and business. As a servant of God, you are not permitted to be involved in an accident because you are divinely protected. Your children will go to school and come back safe because they are covered. You drive out every day and drive back without experiencing evil. Sometimes you hear about a bad thing happening in a place you just left and you wonder, yes, because the mighty hand of God is over you, because you serve him.

10. Peace and security.

When you serve God, you experience peace and security. You can't be in God's service and live in fear, anxiety, and worry. You have peace when you serve the king of heaven because he is committed to your affairs. God will always look after you as you look after his business. He will not allow the wicked to come near you. When you serve God, you will not fear no matter any evil you see happening around you because you are in the hand and covering of the awesome God; you will sleep like a baby because he keeps you in the palm of his hand. I have never seen any true servant of God that lives in fear.

I read a story of one servant of God who, when armed robbers came to his neighborhood, put his tithe booklet at his door and went to sleep. The armed robbers robbed everyone in that neighborhood except his house. One of the robbers actually came to his door, but he heard others arguing and telling him to leave that particular house. This is what happens when you serve God; you are kept secure from trouble. You see, the brother actually went to sleep because he can't serve God with his finances and be living in fear. It is only those who are not servants who will be jittery in that kind of situation. They will call the pastor to pray and may even hold an emergency prayer session. But when you are a servant, you can rest assured that God your employer, who never sleeps, is committed to your peace and security so you can go to sleep in the midst of the storm.

EPILOGUE

MALACHI 3:18

Then shall ye return, and discern between the righteous and the wicked, between him that serveth God and him that serveth him not.

There is coming a shift in this end time when the wealth of this world will come into the hands of the children of God. People who were counted as nothing shall be the ones in control. There will be a transference of wealth from the hands of the wicked to the children of God, but I must tell you this will only manifest in those who serve God. God will soon set apart those who serve him. Those who have been mocked and ridiculed as carrying God's work too much on their head are those that will be distinguished and sought after in their field of endeavor. Therefore, if you are serving, continue because the world will soon hear of you. We are in the last days of the last; the world is coming to an end. There is an impending holocaust on the earth but in the midst of this, there are those who will be shining and succeeding and flourishing to the point that people will begin to seek after them to know their secret, and the secret is in service to God.

Also, God will bless you to the extent that you know. Many people have served God without receiving any blessing from God because they are not aware that what they do attracts blessings. In this kingdom, all you need is knowledge. The Bible says that God's people perish for lack of knowledge.

HOSEA 4:6

> My people are destroyed for
> lack of knowledge...

You can be in church for many years and be involved in all the activities without anything tangible to show as a reward for those services because you are ignorant. If you don't know that you are supposed to be blessed working for God, even when the blessing comes you will not know it is a blessing and that it comes from God based on your services to him. Jacob was in a place without knowing that God was there, so you can serve without knowing there is a reward. This man Jacob slept like a baby on a rock without knowing that place was the very steps to heaven (Genesis 28:11-16).

THE SPIRIT OF SERVANTHOOD

I was discussing with a young lady in our church one day and she told me how she used to drive the van in her former church to pick up members early in the morning for church service and she did that for many years until she left the church. She was not blessed and things did not change in her life. Now that she had joined another church, she got knowledge that anything you do for God attracts his blessing and with this knowledge, she started experiencing blessings in every little thing she did in God's house now.

So to experience God's blessing, you must know that you are entitled to it. The senior brother of the prodigal son in the Bible did not know that he was entitled to everything the father owns and so he never maximized the father's wealth. That is why he got envious when the father threw a party and slew a calf for the brother who just returned from squandering his own portion of the wealth (Luke 15:11-32).

The spirit of servanthood is a must for every believer if you want to excel in life and ministry. This spirit will help you to serve God acceptably. It is the spirit that helped Jesus in his earthly ministry and that is why he succeeded and you too can. The spirit of servanthood will make you humble and make you treat people right in your place of assignment no matter how highly placed you are. To me, this is one of the vital spirits to be engaged for your service in the kingdom.

BOOKS BY THE AUTHOR

WAR IN THE
HEAVENS
*An Exposition Into
Strategic Spiritual Warfare*

THE SPIRIT OF
SERVANTHOOD

Note from the Publisher

Are you a first time author?

Not sure how to proceed to get your book published?
Want to keep all your rights and all your royalties?
Want it to look as good as a Top 10 publisher?
Need help with editing, layout, cover design?
Want it out there selling in 90 days or less?

Visit our website for some exciting new options!

www.chalfant-eckert-publishing.com

If you have been blessed, impacted or given your life to Jesus through reading this book, please let me know through the following means:

victoransor@gmail.com
Twitter: @victoransor
Facebook: Victor Ansor

God Bless You.

www.ingramcontent.com/pod-product-compliance
Lightning Source LLC
Chambersburg PA
CBHW030328080526
44584CB00012B/759